Contents

Chapter 1 – Basic Tools — 2

Chapter 2 – Selections — 13

Chapter 3 – Cloning — 19

Chapter 4 – Working with Layers — 26

Chapter 5 – Effects — 34

Chapter 6 – Vector Graphics — 41

Chapter 7 – Text Effects — 48

Chapter 8 – Optimising Images — 58

Index — 64

Chapter 1
Basic Tools

Getting started

Jasc Paint Shop Pro is a powerful art package which you can use to paint, write text, retouch photos and make images ready for the web. After only a few lessons you will be creating amazing pictures and effects.

Let's get started!

 Load Jasc Paint Shop Pro 7. You can do this in one of two ways:

 Either double-click the Paint Shop Pro icon

 Or click **Start** at the bottom left of the screen, then click **Programs**. When the programs pop up click:

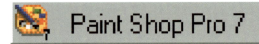

The Opening Screen

▶ Your screen will look like the one below:

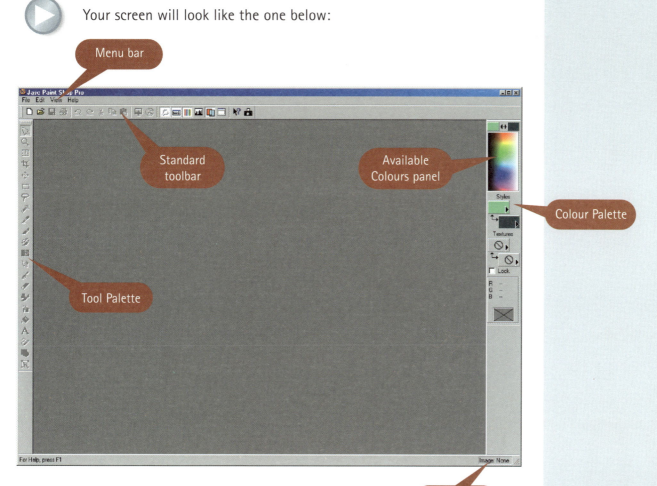

Figure 1.1: The Opening Screen

▶ Just below the **Menu bar** at the top of the screen is the **Standard toolbar**. This has icons which may be clicked instead of choosing common options from the menu.

▶ Down the left side of the screen is the **Tool Palette**. This allows you to use a great variety of effects, filters, paint brushes and spray cans to dramatically enhance your pictures.

▶ Down the right side you'll see the **Colour Palette**. This allows you to set the foreground and background colours. It also allows you to pick styles and textures.

▶ The **Status bar** gives you colour and image size information.

The Standard toolbar

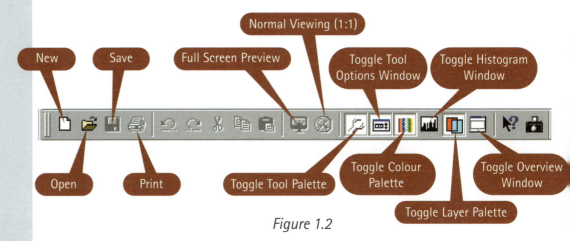

Figure 1.2

Some of the tools on the Standard toolbar such as **New**, **Open**, **Save** and **Print** should be familiar to you.

Try clicking the tools that toggle the various palettes and windows. Be sure to leave the **Tool Palette** and the **Colour Palette** visible on the screen. The other windows you can open when you need them.

Creating a new image

 Choose **File**, **New**, and the **New Image** window appears.

 Set the **Width** and **Height** to 500 pixels and the resolution to 72 pixels (dots) per inch.

 Set the **Background** colour to **Blue**. This is the most suitable colour for the image you are going to create.

The **Image type** default is set to **16.7 Million Colours**. Leave this, and click **OK**.

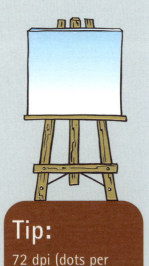

Tip:
72 dpi (dots per inch) is the norm for most computer screens. But if you need to print something it may need to be a higher resolution.

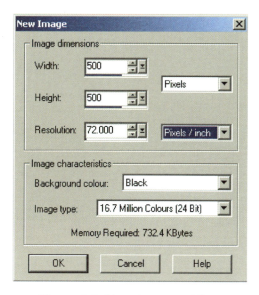

Figure 1.3: New Image settings

 Click **OK**.

Your screen will look like this:

Figure 1.4: Blue Image

If the Title bar says **Image1 [1:2]** this means the picture is zoomed out. Click the **Normal Viewing [1:1]** button on the Standard toolbar.

First we will save our new image.

 Click **File** on the Menu bar and select **Save As**. Under **File name** save it as **Sweets** and ensure the **Save as type** is on the setting **Paint Shop Pro Image**. Click **Save**.

 Now let's go ahead and explore Paint Shop Pro's possibilities on our fresh new blue background.

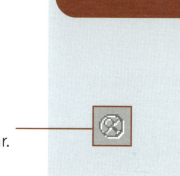

Tip:
It is important to save your work at regular intervals and to be sure that you do not lose too much if something unexpected happens such as a power cut or Artistic Tantrum!

The Tool Palette

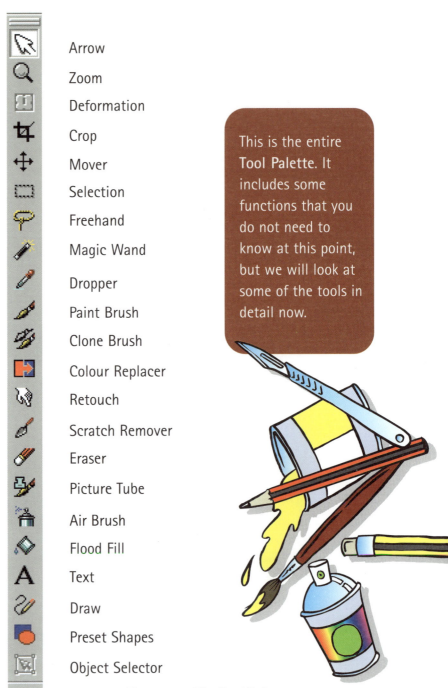

- Arrow
- Zoom
- Deformation
- Crop
- Mover
- Selection
- Freehand
- Magic Wand
- Dropper
- Paint Brush
- Clone Brush
- Colour Replacer
- Retouch
- Scratch Remover
- Eraser
- Picture Tube
- Air Brush
- Flood Fill
- Text
- Draw
- Preset Shapes
- Object Selector

This is the entire **Tool Palette**. It includes some functions that you do not need to know at this point, but we will look at some of the tools in detail now.

Figure 1.5: The Tool Palette

The Paint Brush

▶ The **Paint Brush** is a painting tool. The width of the brush, the amount and density of the paint on the brush, and how it behaves all depend on settings in the **Tool Options** window.

▶ Left click the **Paint Brush** icon.

▶ If the **Tool Options** window is not displayed on your screen, click the **Toggle Tool Options Window** button on the Standard toolbar.

Enter the settings as shown in Figure 1.6.

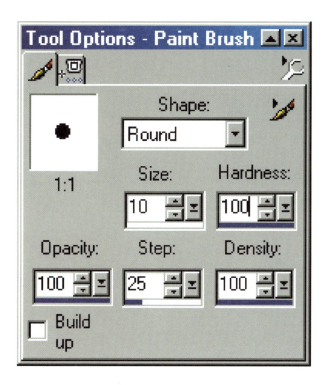

Figure 1.6: The Tool Options window for the Paint Brush tool

 You can move the Tool Options window out of the way by dragging its title bar.

 Try writing your name and also try drawing circles and putting a dot in the middle.

 To change the colour of the brush move your mouse cursor over the Available Colours panel in the Colour Palette and your cursor will automatically change to a dropper icon.

As you move the Dropper icon over the available colours, the selected colour appears in the New Colour Swatch at the bottom of the colour Palette.

 Left-click to select a new colour. Try doodling on the screen with different colours.

Tip:
You can right-click the tool you are using to display its **Tool Options** window.

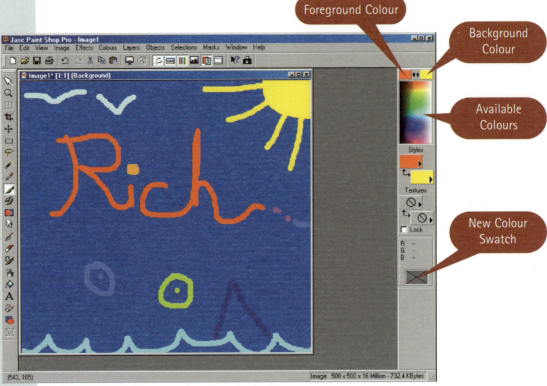

Figure 1.7

Foreground and background colours

When you run the dropper over the **Available Colours** in the Colour Palette and left-click, you are selecting a new **foreground** colour. If you right-click instead, you select a new **background** colour. The colours appear in the two swatches at the top of the Colour Palette.

You can paint with the background colour by dragging with the right mouse button instead of the left. Try it!

The Dropper tool

If you want to paint another line with exactly the same colour you used, say, for the sun in the picture above, you need the **Dropper** tool. Left-click it and then left-click the sun on your canvas. The foreground colour changes to the colour of the sun.

Or, you can right-click with the **Dropper** tool to change the background colour. Then select the **Paint Brush** tool again and paint in either the Foreground or Background colour.

Tip:
You can swap foreground and background colours in the two swatches by clicking the two-head arrow between them.

Undoing mistakes

If you don't like the last line you painted, you can undo it by clicking the **Undo** button.

Or, you can undo a whole lot of strokes using **Edit, Command History**. This brings up a window like Figure 1.8:

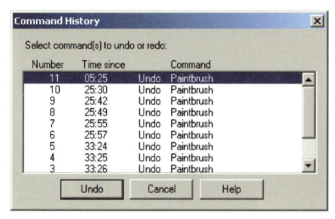

Figure 1.8: Undoing commands

You cannot undo just command number 3, for example. You can undo every command back to a selected number.

You can redo the commands by clicking the **Redo** button on the Standard toolbar.

 Delete some or all of the strokes you have made.

Setting tool options

 Experiment with the **Tool Options** window. The settings shown below produce a quite different effect!

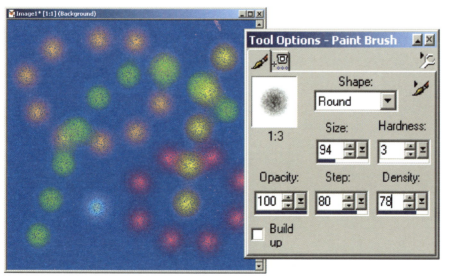

Figure 1.9

Tip:
Try changing Opacity too... reducing Opacity is like adding water to your paintbrush - some of the background shows through.

The Airbrush

 The **Airbrush** is almost the same as the **Paintbrush** and you choose your colours in the same way. The main difference is that if you hold the airbrush in one spot, more colour is deposited.

 Select the **Airbrush** and set the options as shown below.

 It has much softer edges like a spray would be. Have a go with it. Spray circles over each other to make a blancmange effect as in Figure 1.10.

> **Tip:**
> Remember: when colouring in, you can left-click for foreground colour and right-click for background colour. Try reducing **Opacity** for a softer effect.

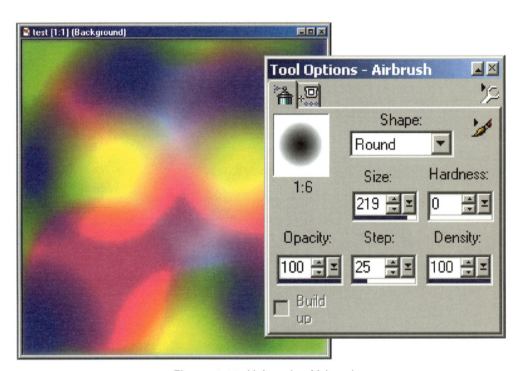

Figure 1.10: Using the Airbrush

The Picture Tube

 The **Picture Tube** is probably the most fun tool in the whole package. Let's have a go with it. Click the **Picture Tube** icon.

You will notice first the **Tool Options** window has completely changed. Let's assume that the picture you now have is a blancmange. Let's find some sweets to garnish it.

 Have a look at the new **Tool Options** window.

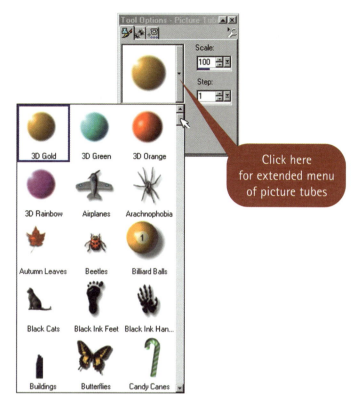

Figure 1.11

▶ Use your cursor and open the extended menu of picture tubes. Select a tube you wish to use. I suggest using candy corn, sweets and jellybeans.

▶ Once a tube has been selected, click your cursor over your canvas as many times as you wish to produce the image.

▶ Go back to the menu to select another tube and repeat the process.

If you don't like the arrangement of sweets you can either go to **File** and press **Revert** which loads your last saved canvas or use **Edit**, **Undo** which will take you back one step.

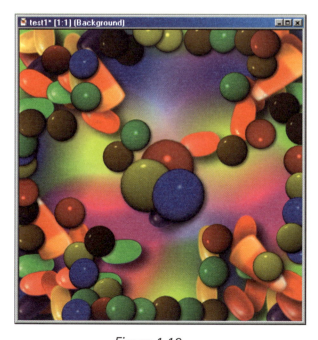

Figure 1.12

Tip:
Change the Scale and Step options and see what happens.

Printing

Before you print it is wise to select **Print Preview** so that you know what the printout will look like.

 From the **File** menu select **Print Preview**. Click **Setup** to bring up the dialogue box shown below.

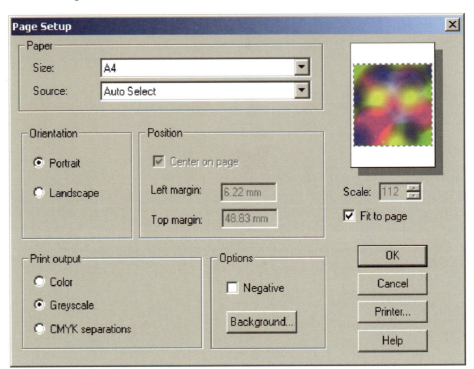

Figure 1.13: The Page Setup dialogue box

 You can select **Center on Page** and other options before printing.

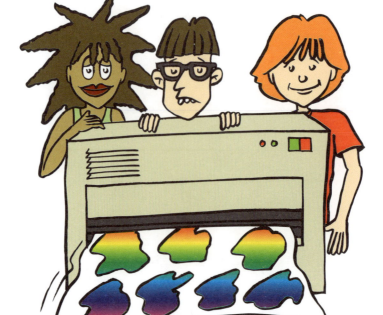

Of course you will need a colour printer to make it worth printing the work of art you have created!

Chapter 2
Selections

Making selections

A selection masks off an area so that you can paint it, move it, copy it or fill it with special effects.

There are three basic tools for making selections.

   The Selection tool

   The Freehand tool

   The Magic Wand tool

The Selection tool

The Selection tool enables you to make selections using different shapes. We'll try it out.

   Open a new canvas with dimensions 500x500 pixels, resolution 72 pixels per inch, 16.7 million colours and a white background.

   Make sure the Title bar says Image1 [1:1] (Background). If it says Image1 [1:2] (Background) you are 'zoomed out' and you will have a very small working area. In that case click the Normal Viewing (1:1) button. ────────────

   Click the Selection tool.

The Tool Options window for the Selection tool may already be open. If it is not, right-click the Selection tool and click on Tool Options.

Drawing with the Selection tool

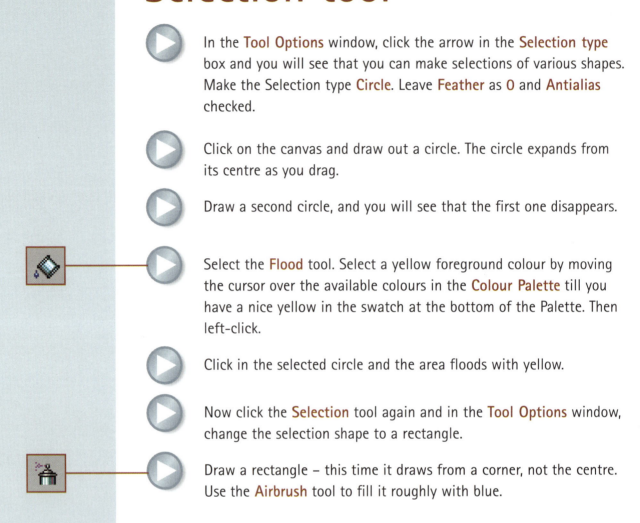

▶ In the **Tool Options** window, click the arrow in the **Selection type** box and you will see that you can make selections of various shapes. Make the Selection type **Circle**. Leave **Feather** as **0** and **Antialias** checked.

▶ Click on the canvas and draw out a circle. The circle expands from its centre as you drag.

▶ Draw a second circle, and you will see that the first one disappears.

▶ Select the **Flood** tool. Select a yellow foreground colour by moving the cursor over the available colours in the **Colour Palette** till you have a nice yellow in the swatch at the bottom of the Palette. Then left-click.

▶ Click in the selected circle and the area floods with yellow.

▶ Now click the **Selection** tool again and in the **Tool Options** window, change the selection shape to a rectangle.

▶ Draw a rectangle – this time it draws from a corner, not the centre. Use the **Airbrush** tool to fill it roughly with blue.

Figure 2.1: Selecting and filling shapes

Tip:
The black and white border around a selection is called a marquee. Sometimes it is referred to as the "marching ants".

Copying and pasting a selection

Your blue square should still be selected.

▶ From the **Edit** menu select **Copy** or click the **Copy** button. ─────

▶ From the **Edit** menu select **Paste**. In the pop-up menu click **As New Selection**. The square is copied into the middle of the canvas.

▶ As it is still selected you can move it. Click the **Mover** tool and ─── move it clear of the circle.

▶ Repeat the **Paste** operation to paste another blue square. Leave it overlapping the yellow circle.

▶ Airbrush the square with a selection of blue and purple shades, leaving no white areas.

You can clear all selections now.

▶ From the **Selections** menu choose **Select None**.

Tip: **Ctrl-D** is a shortcut to Deselect All.

The Magic Wand tool

Using the Magic Wand tool you can select an area of a particular colour. You can set the Tolerance level so that colours which are almost but not quite the same will be selected.

▶ Click the **Magic Wand** tool and then click in the yellow circle.

The portion of the circle not overlapped by the rectangle will be selected.

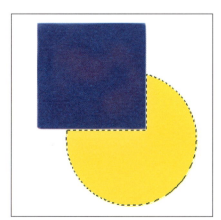

Figure 2.2: Selecting with the Magic Wand tool

Setting the Tolerance level

You could select the square in Figure 2.2 using the **Selection** tool, but we will experiment with setting the Tolerance level of the Magic Wand.

 In the **Tool Options** for the **Magic Wand**, set the Tolerance level to 0.

 Click in the blue square. Probably only a small portion of it will be selected.

 Keep increasing the Tolerance level and clicking in the square.

When you have set the Tolerance level sufficiently high, the whole square will be selected when you click in it. It won't work if you have left any white showing.

Adding selections

Now suppose you wanted to select the circle in addition to the square already selected. You add to selections by keeping the **Shift** key pressed while you make another selection.

 Keep the **Shift** key pressed and click in the circle.

 You can close this image without saving – that's enough practice!

The Freehand tool

We will put some of our new skills to the test by drawing a pattern of flowers using the **Selection** and **Airbrush** tools.

 Open a new canvas, and specify a green background.

 Select the **Freehand Tool** by clicking the tool icon and then place your cursor on the canvas. By dragging the cursor, draw a flower shape as in Figure 2.3. Don't forget you can have as many goes as you like to get it right. Just click **Selections** on the Menu bar and click on **Select None**. This will deselect the flower so you can now draw another flower shape.

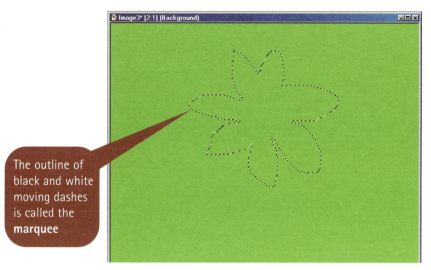

The outline of black and white moving dashes is called the **marquee**

Figure 2.3

Tip:
Don't worry if you draw a wobbly line or spray the wrong colour, just undo using **Ctrl-Z** and try again. Practice makes perfect!

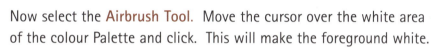

▶ Now select the **Airbrush Tool.** Move the cursor over the white area of the colour Palette and click. This will make the foreground white. Move the cursor over to the canvas, click and colour in the petals.

White foreground

▶ On the **Selection** menu click **Select None**. You can now draw the next part of your picture or draw the petals again if you are not happy with them.

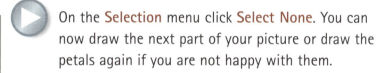

▶ In the **Tool Palette** click on the **Selection** button. In the **Tool Options** window select **Circle**.

▶ Draw a circle in the middle of the flower. Click on the **Airbrush** and spray yellow in the circle selection. Deselect when you have finished colouring.

Tip:
You can use the shortcut Ctrl-D to deselect.

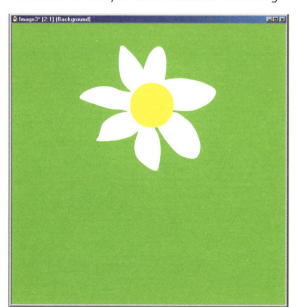

Figure 2.4

Hopefully you will have a flower like this! Now we are going to select the daisy and copy and paste it all over the canvas.

Pasting daisies

▶ Click the **Magic Wand** tool and select the yellow centre.

▶ Keep **Shift** held down while you click in the white part of the flower to select it. You may have to click in several petals if your yellow circle overlaps them.

▶ Click the **Copy** button to copy the selection. Then select **Edit**, **Paste** and choose **As New Selection** from the pop-up menu.

▶ Move the new daisy where you want it.

▶ You can press **Ctrl-Y** to repeat the Paste operation as many times as you like, placing each daisy in a good position.

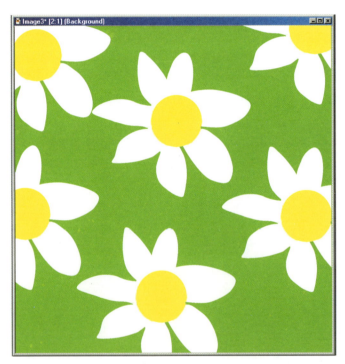

Figure 2.5

▶ Save your picture as **Daisies**.

▶ Try creating some other masterpieces!

Chapter 3
Cloning

Cloning

The Clone brush tool is a very powerful tool and one of the most used implements in the world of professional photo retouchers and computer artists.

You'll need to spend some time playing around with it to understand how it works.

 Open a new canvas, 500 x 500 pixels and specify a blue background.

We are going to make a clown's face, something like the one in Figure 3.1. We will start with the clown's nose.

Figure 3.1

 On the **Tool Palette**, click the **Selection** tool and use the circle selection to draw a circle in the middle of the canvas.

 Choose the **Airbrush** and set the brush size to 50. Spray the nose red.

 Then pick a darker red and carefully spray a shadow area at the bottom of the nose. I would set the **Opacity** to 30 before you start to spray the shadow so you can build the colour up without overdoing it.

Note:
Opacity determines how thickly the paint is laid on. The higher the opacity, the thicker the paint.

Tip:
Remember you can press Ctrl-Z or use the **Undo** button to undo an action and try again!

Note:
Don't forget to customise your airbrush for each selection you spray.

 Now make your airbrush size larger, to about 65, and spray a white highlight. Look at Figure 3.2 for inspiration.

Figure 3.2

 Now click on the **Selection** tool. Select **Ellipse** in the **Tool Options** window and draw an eye shape on the left side of the face. Have a look at Figure 3.3 to see what you are going to create.

 Colour the ellipse white.

 Deselect **(Ctrl-D)** and draw another circle to make the pupil. Colour it black.

 Deselect and spray a white highlight in the pupil. For the highlight set the brush size to 18 and the opacity to 100.

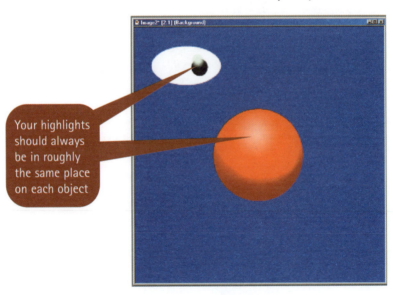

Your highlights should always be in roughly the same place on each object

Figure 3.3

Using the Clone Brush tool

Using the **Clone Brush** tool you can paint an exact copy of any part of an image, either on a new canvas or on another part of the same canvas.

There are three stages to using the Clone Brush tool:

- Set the **Tool Options**
- Activate the **Clone Brush** by right-clicking the image at the position you want to clone
- Position the cursor where you want to start copying, left-click and drag. You will see a crosshair on the original image to show exactly what portion is being copied.

Now give it a go!

Tip:
This tool can only be used on 16 million colour and greyscale images.

 Click the **Clone Brush** tool and set the **Tool Options** as shown in Figure 3.4.

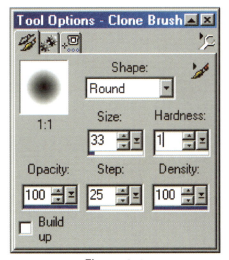

Figure 3.4

 Right-click somewhere in the clown's eye to activate the **Clone Brush**.

 Position the cursor on the right side of the face and start dragging it in small circles to clone the eye.

Figure 3.5: Starting to clone the eye

 Finish cloning the eye.

If the eye is in the wrong position this will give you a chance to practise moving a selection.

Moving a selection

The eye in Figure 3.5 is too high, and needs to be moved.

 Set the background colour to black by right-clicking black on the **Colour Palette**.

When the whole eye is selected, the **Selection** tool changes shape to that of the **Mover** tool as it passes over the selection. If you move the eye now by dragging it, it will leave behind a 'hole' in the background colour.

Try it as follows:

 Use the **Magic Wand** to select the white part of the right eye. Then hold down **Shift** while you select the pupil.

 Now move the eye. You should see something like Figure 3.6.

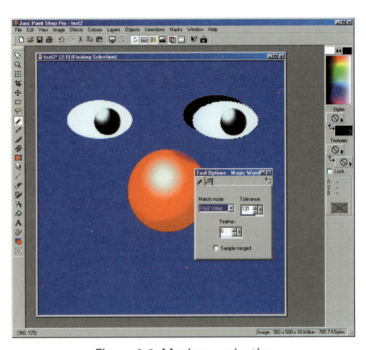

Figure 3.6: Moving a selection

 Undo the move – we need to change the background to blue before moving the eye.

 From the **Selections** menu choose **Select None**.

 Using the **Dropper** tool, right-click the blue background to set the background colour to blue.

 Now try selecting and moving the eye to the correct position.

Subtracting selections

You already know how to add selections by holding down **Shift** as you make a second or third selection. You can also subtract portions of a selection by holding down the **Ctrl** key.

We will paint the mouth using this technique.

 Draw a large circle selection from the middle of the nose.

 Now hold the **Ctrl** key down and draw another circle starting from the top of the nose or between the eyes.

 The second circle has eaten away at the first circle, giving us a neat mouth shape.

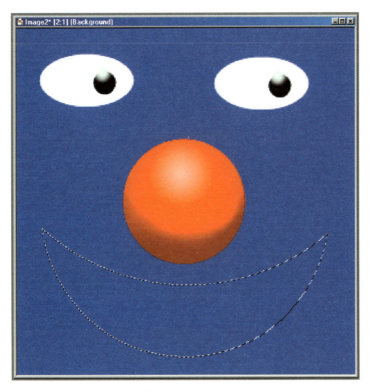

Figure 3.7: Subtracting selections

 Spray the mouth white and, decreasing the opacity to say 10, spray a neat dark blue edge around the bottom of the mouth.

Tip:
When you airbrush fine gradients build them up in fine layers and you will get a much better result.

Modifying a selection

Sometimes the selection area is almost, but not quite, what you want. You can modify it.

 From the Selections menu select Modify. Click Contract.

 Set the Contract Selection window to 12 pixels. Press OK. You should see the selection has got smaller.

 Go back to Selection and Modify and this time go to Feather, set that to 3 pixels. This will give a soft edge to the selection.

 Colour the selection and you should have something that looks like Figure 3.8.

Note the soft edge to the red mouth.

Figure 3.8: A contracted, feathered selection

The Preset Shapes tool

You have learnt a lot about Paint Shop Pro, but there are a lot more fun things hidden away in it.

 Deselect everything and click on the **Preset Shapes** tool on the **Tool Palette**.

Using the **Preset Shapes** tool, add objects to your face. Try different glasses and hairstyles. Make sure **Retain style** is ticked.

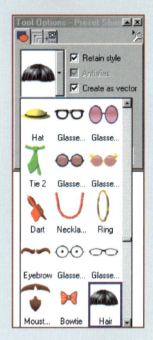

Scale the moustache up or down by clicking the cursor over these small boxes (nodes) around the shape box. You can move the moustache by dragging the centre node

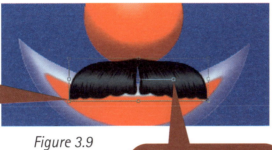

Figure 3.9

You can use this node to rotate the moustache

Does your picture look like mine? If it does then **Undo** using **Ctrl-Z** and try some different glasses or a necklace.

Figure 3.10

Tip:
Use the **Object Selector** tool to move the glasses, hair, bow-tie etc.

25

Chapter 4
Working with Layers

Layers are like transparent sheets layered on top of each other. They can be arranged in different orders, and switched on and off. You can even make the layers react to different colours or contrasts to blend together to make some spectacular pictures.

Supplied with the Paint Shop Pro program CD are some pictures already in digital form. In the next project we will use one of them.

 Open Paint Shop Pro.

 If you have the Paint Shop Pro CD, insert it into the CD drive.

You will see some animated sequences, and finally a menu from which you can select an option.

 Select **Browse CD-ROM**.

 Click the CD drive icon. Select this and look in the **Tutorial Images** folder as shown in Figure 4.1.

You may not have the CD to insert, if you are working on a network. The image you need may be downloaded from **www.payne-gallway.co.uk/psp** and stored in a suitable folder.

 To find an image stored in the computer, from the **File** menu select **Browse**. You'll see a screen similar to Figure 4.1.

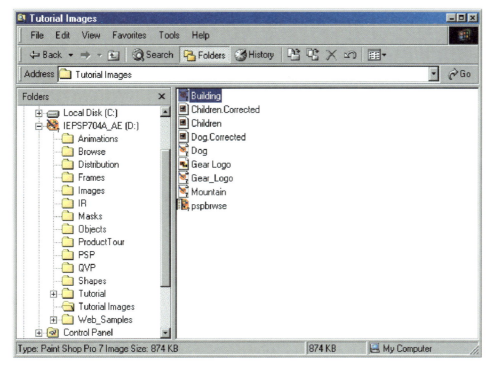

Figure 4.1: Browsing to find an image

- Choose **Building.psp** by double-clicking its icon.

- Make sure **Normal Viewing (1:1)** is selected. (The **Normal Viewing** button should be depressed.)

Figure 4.2

We are going to replace the lake with a lawn and add a sky. We need to think about perspective and shadow direction for maximum artistic effect.

Selecting an area

 OK, click the **Freehand** icon on the **Tool Palette**.

 In the **Tool Options** box set the **Selection type** as **Point to Point** and set **Feather** to **1**.

 Left-click in the top left corner of the water area. When you want to change direction, left-click. When you get back to the first position, right-click to close the box. If you make an error, you will need to close the box before you can use the **Ctrl-Z** feature to start again.

Tip:
The **Feather** option slightly blurs the selection line and helps to blend in your retouching. **Antialias** is a digital enhancer that makes the edges on selections and type much neater.

Adding layers

Each update will be added on a separate layer.

 From the **Layers** menu select **New Raster Layer**.

 You should now see the **Layer Properties** window. Name the layer **grass**.

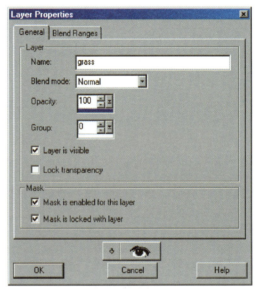

Figure 4.3

 Click **OK**.

Tip:
Another name for Raster layer is Bit-mapped layer.

 You need to be able to see the **Layer Palette**. If it is not on your screen, click the **Toggle Layer Palette** button on the toolbar. In **Roll-up** mode, this toolbar automatically 'rolls up' so that only the Title bar is visible unless the cursor is over it.

 Move the cursor over the **Layer Palette**. Does it have your new layer called **grass** in it?

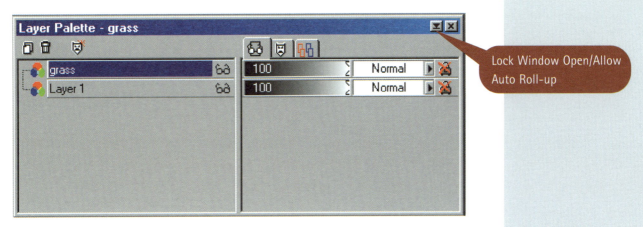

Figure 4.4: The Layer Palette

Painting the lawn

▶ Now select the **Picture Tube** icon and in the library of the **Tube options** select the **Lawn** tube.

▶ Paint in the lawn.

Tip: As you paint the lawn, alter the size of the grass from scale 40 in the distance up to scale 150 in the foreground. Remember, the further away an object is, the smaller it appears.

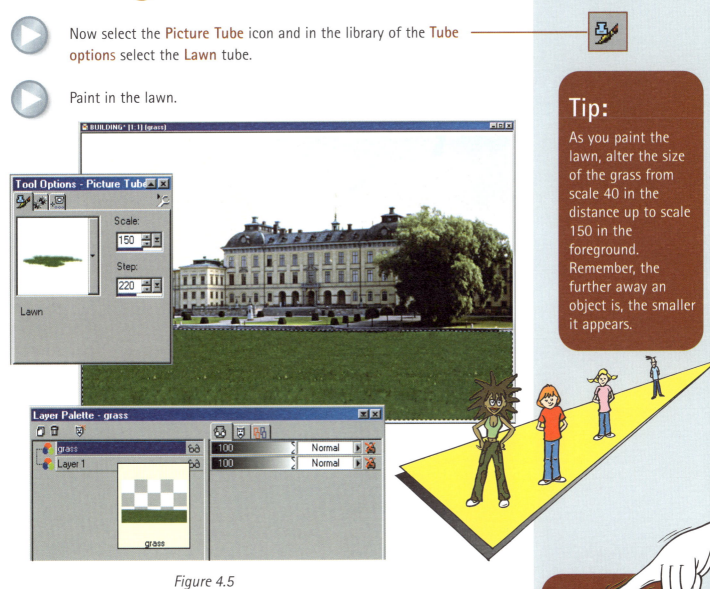

Figure 4.5

Lock Window Open/Allow Auto Roll-up

Run your cursor over the layer "grass" and a small preview window appears.

Painting the dandelions

▶ Make a new **Raster Layer** and call it **dandelion**.

▶ Again using the **Picture Tube** icon select **Dandelion** and paint different sized dandelion flowers, getting larger as they get closer to you.

▶ Make another new layer. This time try using the **Create Layer** icon on the **Layer Palette**.

▶ Call the new layer **dandelion shadows**.

▶ On this new layer, use the **Airbrush** to spray black shadows under the dandelions, trying to make them about the same size as the flowers.

Right-click to zoom up, left-click to go back.

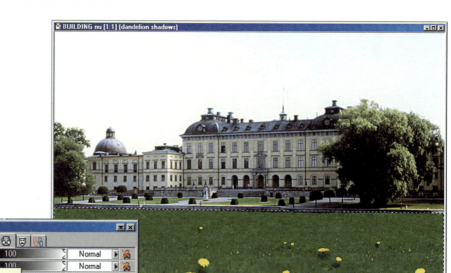

Figure 4.6

▶ The black blobs don't look too much like shadows, but they will once we re-shuffle the layers and place the shadow layer under the dandelion layer.

▶ In the **Layer Palette** click on the **dandelion shadows** layer and drag it to below the **dandelion** layer. The layers should now be rearranged.

This is a good time to look at the options in the **Layer Palette** box.

Layer options

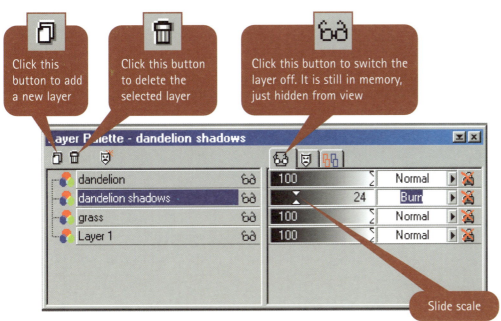

Figure 4.7: The Layer Palette

On the right-hand side of the Layer Palette are more options.

 Change your layer options to match mine. In the dandelion shadows Layer set the Layer Blend Mode to Burn and then using the slide scale, decrease the Opacity until the shadows under the dandelions look realistic.

Figure 4.8

Tip:
Try all the different blend settings. The **Burn** option will darken the grass on the layer below your shadow in a realistic manner, but only if you decrease the opacity first.

Tip:
If your shadows need tweaking a bit you can spray more on or use the **Eraser** tool to refine the shape. If nothing happens, check to see the correct layer is selected.

Tip:
Remember to try to match the darkness of your tree shadow with your dandelion shadow. Also note the direction of the shadows in the picture and try to replicate this.

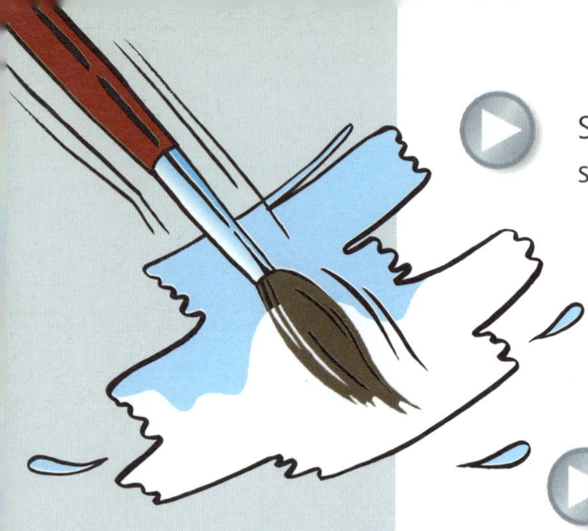

▶ Set your Airbrush to Opacity **20** and Size **60** with black and spray a shadow on the grass under the trees in the distance.

▶ Note how your brush sprays in the blended mode!

▶ Switch the layers on and off to see what a difference you have made.

▶ Change the **Layer Blend Mode** for the grass layer, the effects are much more wild and fun. OK, set it back to **Normal**.

Painting the sky

▶ Click the **Magic Wand** on the **Tool Palette**, and change the **Tool Options** to match mine in Figure 4.9. **Tolerance** is set to **20**, **Feather** is set to **1**.

▶ The **Magic Wand** will select everything of the same colour – perfect for us to make a time-saving selection of the sky.

▶ Click on **Layer 1** in the **Layer Palette**, which has the original image on it, and click the wand in the sky...

As if by magic the sky is selected.

Figure 4.9

▶ Make a new **Raster Layer** and call it **sky**.

- Move it to the top of layer stack.

- Click the **Maximise** icon to give yourself some space around the picture. This makes it easier to spray the sky from edge to edge.

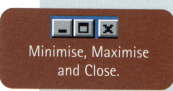
Minimise, Maximise and Close.

- Get a very large airbrush and spray the top part of the sky blue, leaving the area at the bottom white.

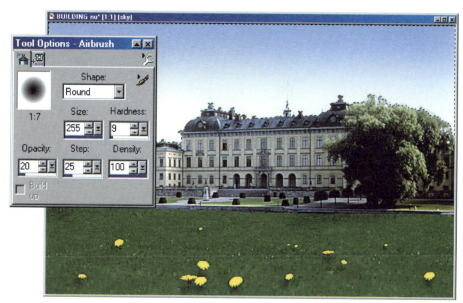

Figure 4.10

- Using the **Picture Tube** select **Clouds** and make them **scale 100**.

- Add them low down in the sky as in Figure 4.11.

- Deselect everything with **Ctrl-D**.

- OK, that should do it. Your first photo re-touching is complete.

Tip:
Skies always get bluer the further up you look.

Figure 4.11

- Well done, save and print out to show the unbelievers.

Chapter 5
Effects

By adding different effects to a picture you can create some spectacular results very quickly. You can also transform a photograph into something quite different! In this chapter you will change a photograph of some snow-clad mountains into a photograph which appears to have been taken on Mars.

Experimenting with effects

We will use a photograph supplied with Paint Shop Pro.

 Open Paint Shop Pro.

 Refer to the beginning of Chapter 4 to see how to find a stored photograph. You need to find the one named **Mountain.psp**. If you have not got the Paint Shop Pro CD, you can download the image from **www.payne-gallway.co.uk/psp**.

Figure 5.1

Changing the hue

Before we start, what do we know about Mars? Do we have any reference? We know it has a red atmosphere with clouds and there are electric storms. The vehicle that went to Mars could only take rather low resolution pictures.

 On the Tool Palette, click the Magic Wand and select the sky. You may need to hold down Shift and click any unselected sky.

 Now paint in clouds using the Picture Tube or freehand with the Airbrush.

We need to give a red hue to the picture (because it is the red planet).

 On the Colours menu select Adjust, Hue/Saturation/Lightness.

 Make sure the Colourize box is ticked. Move the Hue handle to the right until you have a red shade. Then move the Lightness handle down to darken the sky.

The colour change will only affect the selected area. You can see the effect in the right-hand picture.

The settings should be approximately as shown in Figure 5.2.

Tip:
Remember that setting the **Tolerance** to a higher value in the **Tool Options** box allows the Magic Wand to select areas of slightly different colours. If the **Tool Options** box is not displayed, click the **Toggle Tool Options** button on the toolbar.

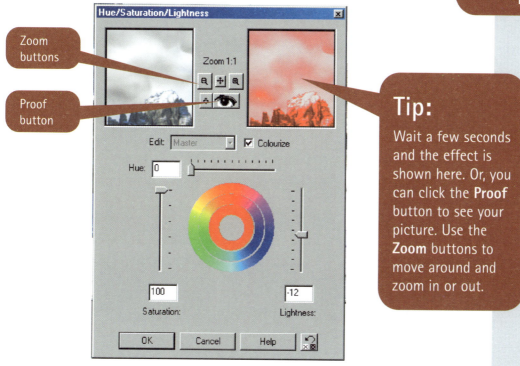

Tip:
Wait a few seconds and the effect is shown here. Or, you can click the **Proof** button to see your picture. Use the **Zoom** buttons to move around and zoom in or out.

Figure 5.2: Changing Hue, Saturation and Lightness

From the **Selections** menu click **Invert** to select the other part of the picture. Darken the landscape a little more than the sky.

Figure 5.3

Zooming in

 You can zoom in on a portion of the picture using the **Zoom** tool.

 Deselect the selected area.

Click the **Zoom** tool and click in the mountain area. Keep clicking, zooming in closer and closer.

 At some point you will see that the image is made up of different coloured squares, called **pixels**.

Figure 5.4: A close-up view of the pixels which make up the picture

When you zoom in, the pixels are shown larger. The more pixels per inch, the higher the resolution.

Remember: You can use the shortcut **Crtl-D** to deselect everything.

This image is 770 pixels wide and 528 high, and the image cannot be viewed any bigger at the set resolution because there is no more information stored. It is a **bitmap** or **raster** image.

There is another type of image called a **vector** image that can be scaled or viewed at any size and you will never see any pixels. You will work with vector images in the next chapter.

▶ Click the **Normal Viewing** button to return to Normal view.

Tip:
You can quickly see the size of your image if you look in the bottom right corner of your program window.

Adding a lightning strike

▶ From the **Layers** menu select **New Raster Layer** to make a new layer. Call it **lightning**. Leave the default options and click **OK**.

▶ Select the **Picture Tube** and in the options you will find **lightning**.

▶ Play about with **Scale** in the **Tool Options** box and try to find a really good lightning strike, keep undoing and reapplying to get the best one.

▶ When you have a really dangerous lightning strike move it horizontally using the **Mover tool** to find the best place, preferably in front of some dark areas for best effect.

Be careful with the mover tool. If you do not click on the lightning accurately the whole picture will move.

▶ Create another new layer. Right-click and rename the new layer **far lightning**.

▶ Draw some smaller lightning strikes in the distance.

▶ From the **Effects** menu select **Blur, Gaussian Blur**. Try the effect of setting the **Radius** to different values. The larger the radius, the more blurred the effect.

▶ Hover the cursor over the **Layer Palette** title bar, which should be visible on your screen, and click **Layer1** to select it. Experiment with blurring the mountain layer to see what happens.

▶ In the **Layer Palette** set your **Layer Blend Mode** to **Dodge** in the **lightning** layer. Looks great, doesn't it!

Tip:
If you feel confident you could draw different lightning strikes along the layer and rub out the ones you don't want using the eraser tool. You can also clip the lightning to look like it's striking the mountain top.

Right-click your foreground lightning layer to select it and in the pop-up menu select **Duplicate**. The new layer will be called **Copy of lightning**.

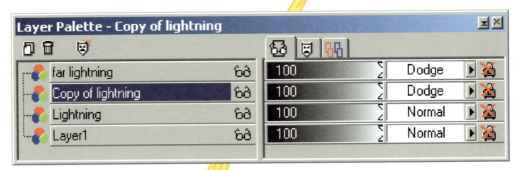

Figure 5.5

 Looking good... select **Layer 1** and from the **Effects** menu select **Illumination Effects**, **Sunburst**.

 Using the **cross** in the left window, make sure the **Sunburst effect** comes from the top of the main lightning strike.

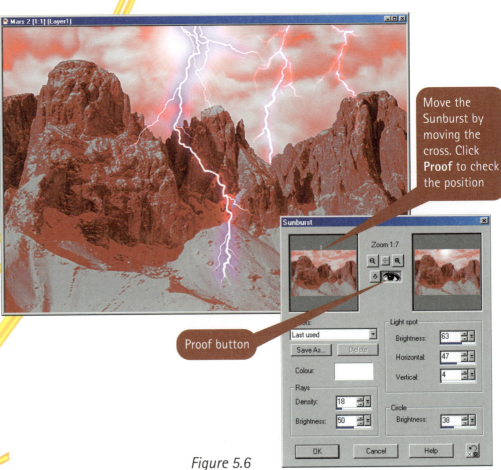

Figure 5.6

 Save the layered version of your picture.

Merging layers

The last effect will be a global effect so we need to merge all the layers.

 From the Layers menu select Merge, Merge All (Flatten).

 In the Layers menu select Duplicate to duplicate the flattened layer. We duplicate the layer so we have a copy of an original to refer to or to start again.

 From the Effects menu select Geometric Effects, Wind and set at strength 6 from the left. Click OK.

 From the Effects menu select Geometric Effects, Spiky Halo, and try my settings in Figure 5.7.

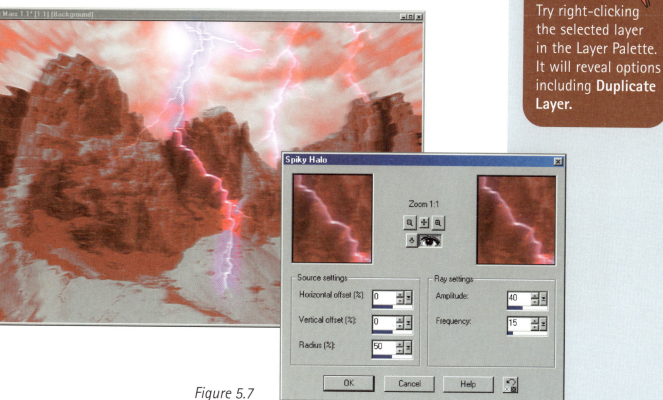

Figure 5.7

Tip:
Try right-clicking the selected layer in the Layer Palette. It will reveal options including **Duplicate Layer.**

The effect is to make it look as if we are peering through a thick glass window.

If you wish you can now turn off the duplicated layer and draw a space ship on the original layer. Then apply the same effects to it to get the thick glass effect. You can do this by using the techniques we used in chapter 2.

Figure 5.8

Note:
I used an elongated ellipse to create my space rocket.

Note:
I used lots of lightning and the warp filter to create my blinding ball of electricity.

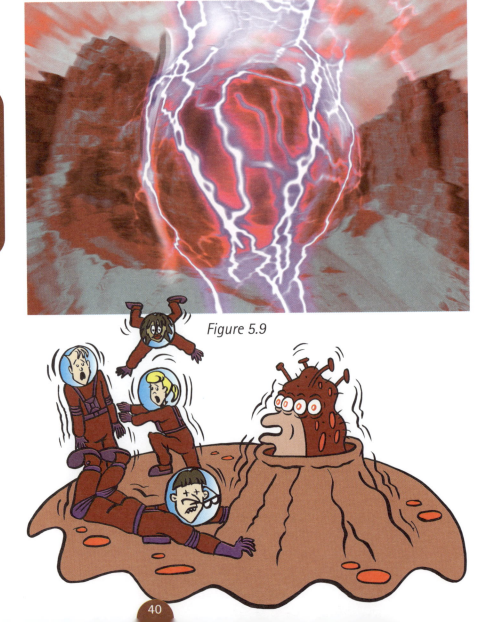

Figure 5.9

Chapter 6
Vector Graphics

Raster or bitmap images are made up from an array of different coloured pixels. The resolution of a picture is measured typically in pixels per inch (ppi) or dots per inch (dpi), and the more pixels per inch, the finer the detail in the picture. Raster images are very good for storing and changing photographic style pictures but if you enlarge the image, the results will probably not be satisfactory and individual pixels will be visible.

Vector images are made from mathematical information about the curves, sizes, and point positions and colours. Whenever you change the size of a vector image, rotate it or skew the image, it is redrawn and will be perfect. This type of image is good for graphical shapes or text. We are now going to create a vector image.

The Great Bear

 Open a new canvas 700 pixels wide and 600 high. Specify a red background, and click **OK**.

 Make the foreground colour black by clicking black in the **Colour Palette**. Set the background style to **Null** in the **Styles** box.

 Click the **Preset Shapes** tool, and select **Ellipse** from the **Tool Options – Preset Shapes** box.

Figure 6.1

The background style is set to **Null** so that the ellipse will not be filled with the background colour automatically

Click the styles arrow and select Null

Draw the first ellipse for the bear's body. It goes off the edge of the canvas as shown in Figure 6.2. You can move it by dragging the centre node, and size it by dragging a node on the box surrounding it.

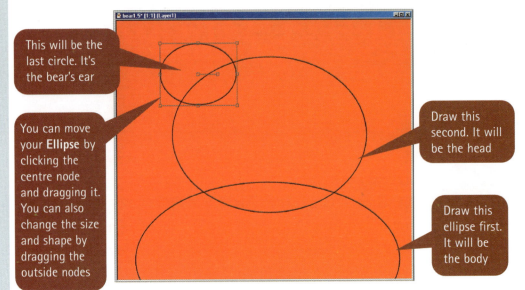

This will be the last circle. It's the bear's ear

You can move your **Ellipse** by clicking the centre node and dragging it. You can also change the size and shape by dragging the outside nodes

Draw this second. It will be the head

Draw this ellipse first. It will be the body

Figure 6.2

 Draw the ellipses for the head and left ear, sizing them and positioning them carefully. You can always click **Ctrl-Z** to undo your last action if it goes wrong.

Copying and pasting objects

  After drawing the ear, click the **Object Selector** (the bottom tool in the **Tool Palette**). Right-click the line of the ear, and select **Copy**.

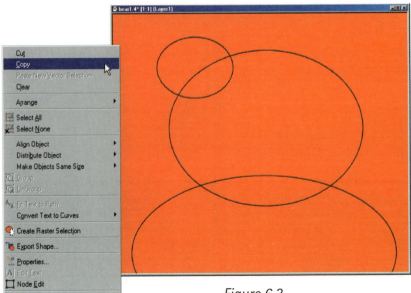

Figure 6.3

Right-click again and click **Paste New Vector Selection**. Move it to the correct position on the other side of the face and left-click.

 Right-click, copy and select **Paste New Vector Selection** again. Another ear shape will appear to make the inside of the ear. Use the corner node to scale it down a little.

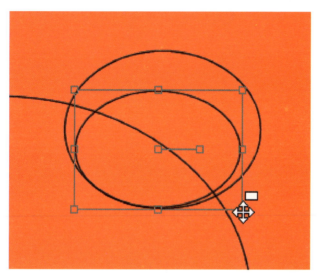

Figure 6.4

 Using **Copy** and **Paste New Vector Selection** put a circle in the other ear.

 Draw some more circles for eyes using the **Preset Shapes Tool Option** again.

Figure 6.5

You will probably find that some of your objects are not quite correctly positioned. Use the **Object Selector** tool to select an object that you want to move. Drag its centre node to move it.

Remember too that you can select several objects at once by holding down **Shift** while you select each one.

 Draw circles to make the bear's eyes, then make the snout and lastly a nose.

Figure 6.6

Selecting a Fill colour and style

Right, let's colour our Vector Bear.

  Start by selecting the body using the **Object Selector** tool.

 In the **Object Selector Tool Options** box, choose **Properties**.

The Vector Properties box opens as in Figure 6.7. The **Stroke** refers to the outline of an object. You can 'stroke' using brushes of different widths, line styles, textures and colours.

The **Fill** can also be in different patterns, textures and colours.

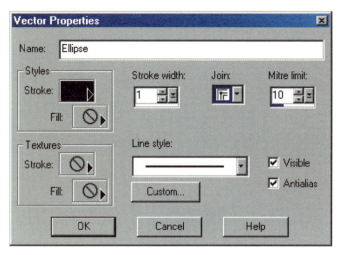

Figure 6.7

 Click **Styles**, and then the black arrow in **Fill**. Choose **Solid** by clicking the first box (the paintbrush).

 Click in the **Fill** box again to choose the colour.

The Colour window

The **Colour** window opens. You can select a colour from the basic Palette of 16 colours, or you can move the little circles either in the square on the right or its surrounding circle to pick a more subtle colour.

Every colour is made up from a combination of red, green and blue. You can also type in values between 0 and 255 for red, green and blue, and values for hue, saturation and light.

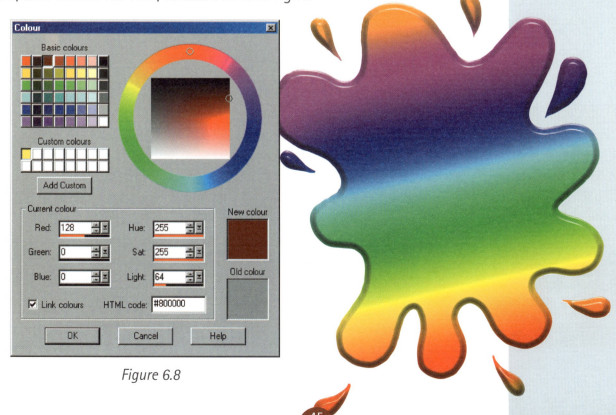

Figure 6.8

45

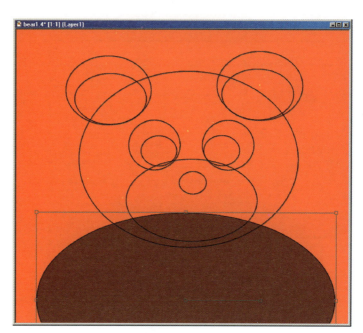

Figure 6.9

I chose a deep burgundy from the basic colours.

> Now drag the **Object Selector** right across the whole head to select all the circles.

> Colour them the same as the body. To do this, select a **Solid Fill** as before in the **Vector Properties** window, and click the icon again in the **Fill** box to bring up the **Colour** window. Then move your cursor into the teddy's body on the canvas. (You may have to move the Vector Properties window and Colour Palette out of the way.) Left-click and the colour will appear in the **New Colour** box. Click **OK**.

> Using the **Object Selector**, select the circles in the ears and the snout.

Tip:
If you draw things in the wrong order, so that for example the nose ends up behind the snout, you can right-click an object, select **Arrange**. Then select **Move Up**, **Move Down** etc.

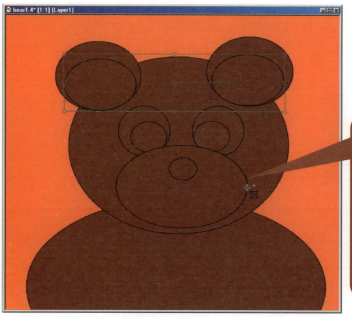

Press **Shift** and, keeping **Shift** depressed, click on the circles to select multiple objects

Figure 6.10

46

Colour these with a pinky fill.

 Colour the eyes white and the nose and pupils black.

Finishing touches

 Click **Preset Shapes** in the **Tool Palette**. Find **Arrow 21**.

 Draw it on and turn it upside down.

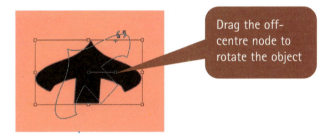

 Deselect, save and print out your first vector picture!

figure 6.11

Finally, check the size in bytes of this image compared with previous images you have saved. You will find that this is much smaller – another advantage of vector graphics!

Chapter 7
Text Effects

Let's look at some funky text projects.

 Open a new red canvas 400 by 80 pixels.

 Choose the **Text** tool and click on the canvas.

 Type **My Web Site** and choose a text style. Keep the size to 40.

 Make the **Stroke** and **Fill** colour yellow. Make sure **Create as Vector** is selected.

Figure 7.1

Tip:
Naming your layers is a great habit to get into.

Click **OK**. Position your text using the centre node and size it using the outside nodes.

Figure 7.2

 In the **Layer Palette**, right-click **Layer 1** and select **Convert to Raster layer** (so we can use the Effects options).

Right-click again and select **Rename**. Name the layer **Words**.

 From the **Effects** menu select **3D Effects**, **Drop Shadow**. Use the settings in Figure 7.3.

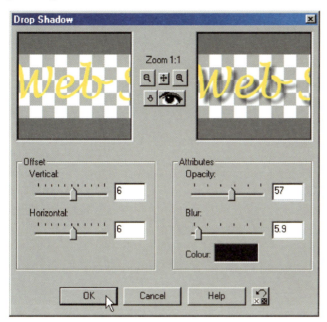

Figure 7.3

 In the **Layer Palette** select the background layer and from the **Effects** menu select **3D Effects**, **Buttonize**. Use the settings in Figure 7.4.

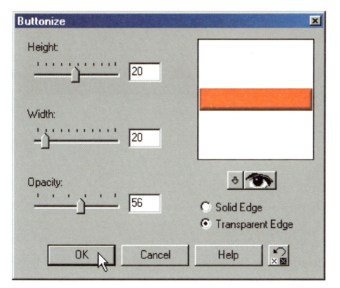

Figure 7.4

 Does it look like my one? Try different text styles and colours. Save your finished picture.

Figure 7.5

Tip:
You could use a customised button like this on your own web site!

Using multiple effects

This time we will use multiple effects (filters) to get great results.

▶ Make a new black background 600 x 150 pixels.

 ▶ Using the **Text** icon write the word "**Chrome**".

 Make the **Styles**, **Fill** box a steel grey colour. The font is Copperplate Gothic Bold, size 65.

Make a capital **C**

Figure 7.6

 Size the text using the nodes so it is nice and big.

Figure 7.7

 Right-click **Layer 1** in the **Layer Palette** and select **Convert to Raster layer**.

 From the **Effects** menu select **Texture Effects**, **Sculpture**. The **Pattern** is set to 2.

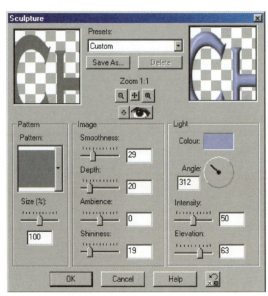

Figure 7.8

From the **Effects** menu select **Artistic Effects**, **Chrome**. Use the settings shown in Figure 7.9 and then click **OK**.

Note:
Copy my settings carefully to get the best result, and experiment to see what happens if you deselect **Use original colour**. Remember you can see the effect of changes by clicking the **Proof** button in the **Chrome** window.

Figure 7.9

 Click the **Background layer** in the **Layer Palette**. Using the **Airbrush**, colour it bright blue.

From the **Effects** menu select **Illumination Effects**, **Sunburst**, using the cross to place it over the top of the H. Keep clicking the **Proof** button and moving the cross till you are satisfied.

Figure 7.10

Tip:
Set the opacity of the Airbrush to about 20 and the size to about 35.

Finally on **Layer 1** in the **Layer Palette**, using the **Airbrush**, spray a little white highlight over the top edge of the character nearest to the sunburst.

Save your masterpiece!

Figure 7.11

A Horror Book cover

This project uses text and effects to make a book cover as spooky as possible. Illustrators often achieve this by making the background very dark and by using eerie light.

 Click on the background colour in the **Colour Palette** and then using the **Colour wheel**, change it to a dark green/blue.

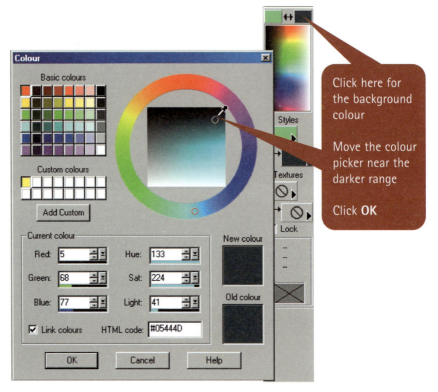

Figure 7.12

 Create a new canvas 550 pixels wide by 800 high. Select **Background colour** in the box.

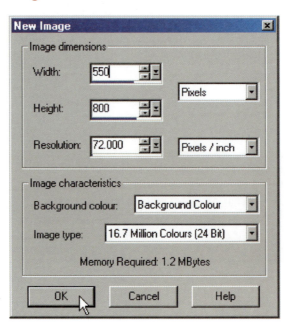

Figure 7.13

Drawing freehand

First of all we will draw some underwater cliffs.

 Click the Freehand tool. In the Tool Options box set Selection type to Freehand and Feather to 5.

 Use the tool to draw a cliff. You will have to draw around the outside of the canvas so that you end up at the same point you started.

 Use a large airbrush (e.g. 250) on a low opacity (e.g. 5) to spray the underwater cliffs a darker green/blue than the background colour.

 Using the Freehand tool again, draw another underwater cliff and make it a little less feathered (3), and then spray just the inside edge of the second underwater cliff. Look at Figure 7.14 to help you.

Tip: Feathering softens the edges – the higher the Feather, the softer the edge.

Tip: Remember to press **Ctrl-D** to deselect before drawing another selection.

Tip: You need to be able to see the whole canvas, so you may need to zoom out using the **View** button.

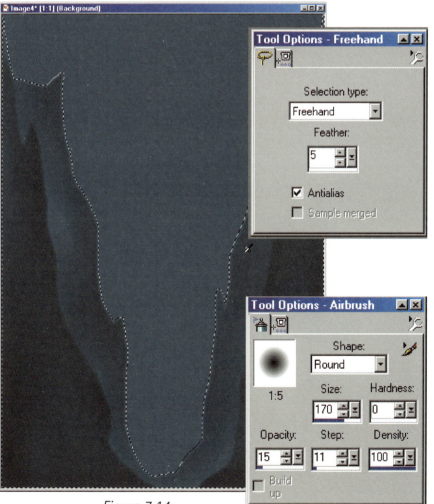

Figure 7.14

▶ Draw a third set of cliffs, with a **Feather** setting of 1 pixel. Making sure the **Airbrush** is set to **Opacity 3**, spray a light covering of the same colour over it.

Tip:
Go to the **Layers** menu to make a new Raster Layer.

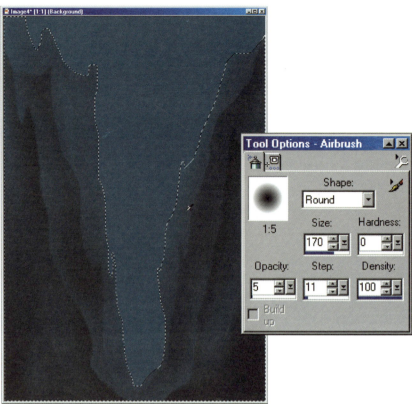

Figure 7.15

▶ Make a new Raster Layer and call it **Eerie Light**. Change the **Eerie Light Layer Blend Mode** to **Dodge**. Using a very large brush, airbrush some white at the bottom of the canyon. Looks pretty eerie doesn't it?

Figure 7.16

Adding text

Next we need to add some text for the book title. The book will be called "The Deep" and be written by you.

 Grab the **Text** tool and click in the picture. Write **The** using **Chiller** text, size 72, as in Figure 7.17. Set the **Fill** colour to a bluish grey.

 Stroke is Null. Choose a bluish grey colour for the fill

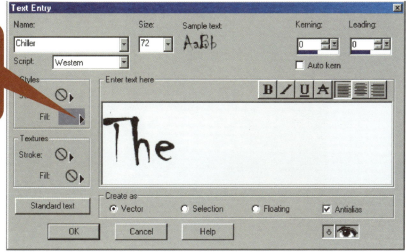

Figure 7.17

 Hit **OK** and click on the canvas again with the **Text** tool. Write **DEEP** and click **OK**.

 Using the **Object Selector** move the Vector text about to get something like Figure 7.18.

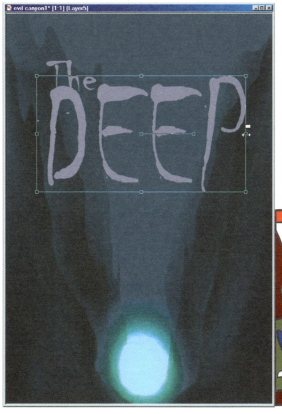

Figure 7.18

In the **Layer Palette**, right-click the vector layer with the text (Layer 2), and select **Convert to Raster Layer**. Right-click again and rename your text layer **the DEEP**.

 From the **Effects** menu select **Geometric Effects**, **Warp**.

> The warp effect makes the text look more like it is underwater.

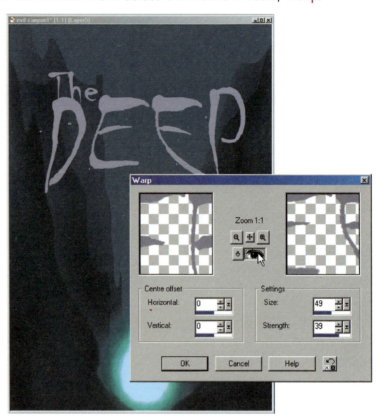

Figure 7.19

 Right-click the text layer **the DEEP** and select **Duplicate**.

 Match the layer blend modes to Figure 7.20.

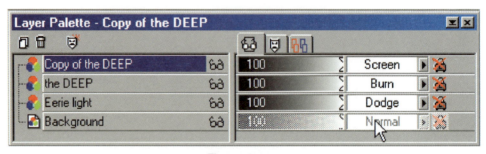

Figure 7.20

 Click the **Mover** tool; by clicking on the text move the top layer to the left and up as Figure 7.22.

In the layer Palette click "**the DEEP**" layer and go to **Effects**, **3D Effects**, **Drop Shadow**, as in Figure 7.21.

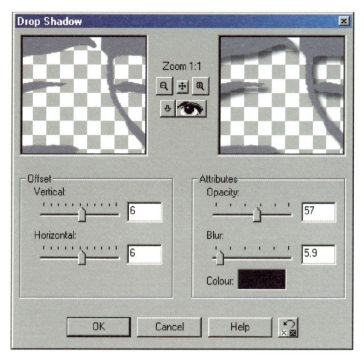

Figure 7.21

▶ Lastly add some more text in a suitable colour, saying **A horror story by** (your name), and place and size it where you think looks cool.

Figure 7.22

Aaaaaaarrghhhhh!

Chapter 8
Optimising Images

Removing red eye

First of all we are going to look at ways of touching up a photograph that you might, for example, want to post on a web site or e-mail to a friend.

You will need the Paint Shop Pro CD, or you can download the image from **www.payne-gallway.co.uk/psp**.

  Open Paint Shop Pro and from the **File** menu select **Browse**. Click the **CD** icon and then **Tutorial Images**. Open **Dog.jpg** by double-clicking the icon.

You will notice that the dog has red eye (or in this case, white eye), a common problem in photography. We will fix it and optimise the picture as a **.jpg** for the web.

  From the **Effects** menu select **Enhance Photo** and pick **Red-eye Removal**.

Figure 8.1

▶ Look in the *right* Red-eye Removal frame. With the hand icon, move the picture so you have an eye central in the window. Zoom in to get a good look at the eye.

▶ You will get a cross hair in the *left* Red-eye Removal frame. Aim it at the centre of the eye and click, holding the mouse button down; draw out until the iris is selected. Finally adjust by using the nodes.

▶ Try the settings as in Figure 8.2. Keep checking with the Proof button till you are satisfied. Select OK.

▶ Now redo the process for the other eye.

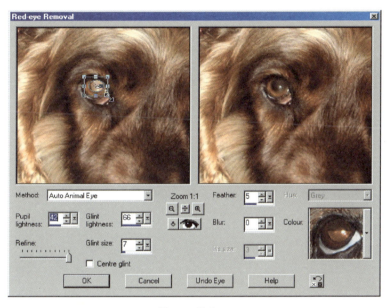

Figure 8.2

▶ Try to remove the dog's scarf using the Clone Brush.

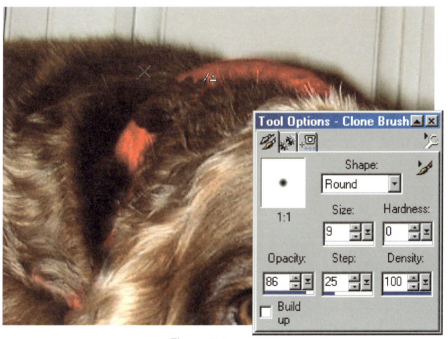

Figure 8.3

Tip:
Remember you can use the Clone Brush to touch up your photos if you scan them into your computer. (Look back to Chapter 3 if you can't remember how to use the Clone Brush.

Optimising for the Web

When you save images to go onto the World Wide Web you need to make sure the file sizes are as small as possible to keep the download times as short as possible.

There are two file formats available for Web pages: GIF and JPEG. Each of these formats compresses the file in a different way, and each format is best for a different type of image. JPEGs (Joint Photographic Experts Group) are best for photographic images. GIF files are good for images like cartoons and simple graphics that have large areas of similar colours. We'll try both formats.

Paint Shop Pro has a very simple method of optimising images for the World Wide Web.

Most people that log onto the web have screen resolutions of 1024 pixels wide and 768 pixels high. So if our picture is 600 pixels wide it will take up over half the screen, quite big enough to look at.

 To make sure the image is not too large, from the **Image** menu elect **Resize**.

Tip:
If you need a specific height, just type it in and the width will change automatically.

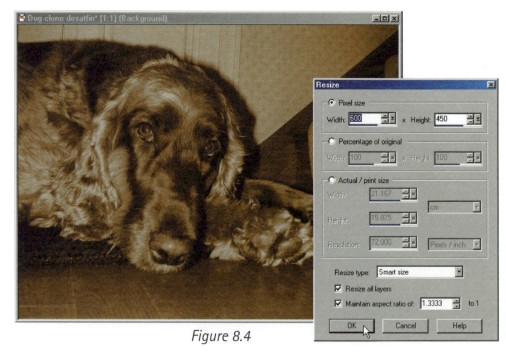

Figure 8.4

 Change the width to 600 pixels wide and the height will change automatically to keep the proportions. Hit **OK**.

 From the **File** menu select **Export**, **JPEG Optimizer**.

Here are the options that you are presented with.

 Set the compression at about **50**. Try moving it to different values between 1 and 100, checking the difference in the Proofing window on the right. When you start to see the image breaking up you have gone too far.

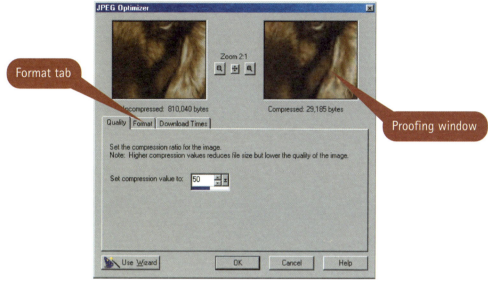

Figure 8.5

 Click the **Format** tab.

As your image downloads you can have it display differently. I think the **Standard** style is cooler.

 Press the **Download Times** bar.

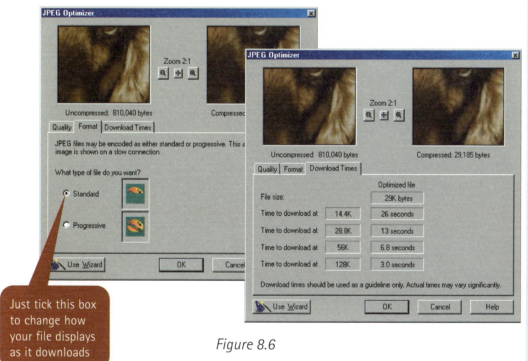

Figure 8.6

This window will show you the size of the file and how long it will take to download. Look at the file size of the uncompressed picture and then look at the compressed version; it really does make a huge difference.

 Press **OK**.

 Save the file and place it in a new folder for your Web pictures.

 When you are finished, close your original dog-retouched picture but don't save your changes.

Creating a .gif file

Finally, we'll look at creating at transforming a simple graphic to a GIF format file suitable for the Web.

 Open your Vector Bear.

 From the **Image** menu select **Resize**. Make this image 600 pixels wide.

Next, from the **File** menu select **Export**, **GIF Optimizer**.

Tip:
If you want to make part of your picture transparent, click **Areas that match this colour**. A picker icon will appear. Click the colour you need transparent, such as the red background, and it will disappear.

Figure 8.8

 Don't worry about **Partial Transparency**. Click **Colours**.

As there are only a few colours in this vector picture, turn the number of colours right down – it will make the file size much smaller.

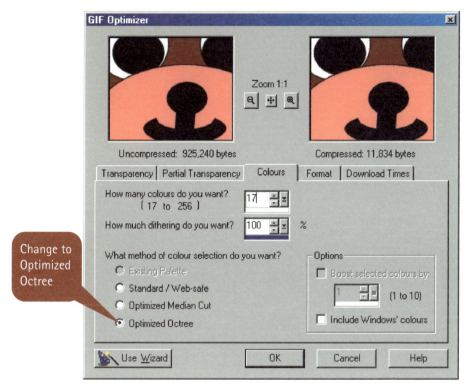

Figure 8.9

 Check the **Format** and **Download Times** as before for the **Dog** picture.

Now you can add a real **splash** of colour to your homework and presentations!

Index

Adding layers	28
Airbrush	10
Antialias	28
Background	
colour	8, 52
layer	51
Bitmap image	37
Clone Brush tool	19, 21, 59
Colour window	45
Colours menu	35
Colour	
Palette	3, 52
selecting	45, 52
wheel	52
window	45
Command History	9
Copying a selection	15
Copying/pasting objects	42
Deselect	15, 33
Download Times	61
dpi	4, 41
Dropper tool	8, 22
Effects	34
menu	49
Export image format	60, 62
Feather	24, 28, 53
Fill	44
Filters	50
Flood tool	14
Foreground colour	8
Freehand tool	13, 16, 28, 53
GIF	60
Illumination effects	38, 51
JPEG	60
Layer	26
adding	28, 30
converting to raster	48
creating	30
deleting	31
duplicating	38
hiding	31
merging	39
naming	28
Options	30
Palette	28, 30, 31
Properties	28
renaming	49
Magic Wand tool	13, 15, 32
Marquee	17
Menu bar	3
Mover tool	22, 56
New Colour Swatch	7
New Image	4
Normal Viewing	27
Object Selector tool	25, 42
Objects	
copying & pasting	42
moving	37, 43
rotating	47
selecting	25, 42, 46
Opacity	19
Optimising for the Web	60
Page Setup	12
Paint Brush	6
Pasting a selection	15, 18, 43
Photographs, enhancing	58
Picture Tube	10, 29, 33, 35
Pixel	4, 36
ppi	41
Preset Shapes tool	25, 41
Print Preview	12
Proof button	35, 38, 59
Raster image	37
Red-eye Removal	58
Redo commands	9
Resize image	60
Resolution	4, 41
Revert	11
Roll-up	28
Saving an image	5
Select None	15
Selection tool	13
Selections	13
adding	16
contracting	24
copying & pasting	15
deselecting	15
inverting	36
menu	15
modifying	24
moving	22, 43
subtracting	23
Solid Fill	46
Standard toolbar	3, 4
Status Bar	3
Stroke	44
Styles box	41
Text tool	48
Tolerance level	16, 35
Tool	
Clone Brush	19, 21, 59
Dropper	8, 22
Flood	14
Freehand	13, 16, 28, 53
Magic Wand	13, 15, 32
Mover	22, 56
Object Selector	25, 42
Picture Tube	10, 29, 33, 35
Preset Shapes	25, 41
Selection	13
Text	48
Zoom	36
Tool Options window	6, 9
Tool Palette	3, 6
Undo commands	9
Vector Graphics	37, 41, 44, 47
Zoom buttons	35, 36